101
LIFE-CHANGING PRINCIPLES

VOLUME I.

DOMINIK PROKOP

101
LIFE-CHANGING PRINCIPLES

VOLUME I.

How to help your children, yourself and others around
you become healthy, happy and successful, and hold
onto great values and ethics.

ISBN: 978-1-7346012-0-6 (Paperback)
Library of Congress Control Number: 2020902937
Front and back cover images by Dominik Prokop.
Book design by Dominik Prokop.

Printed and published in the United States of America.
First printing edition 2020.
Published by 101 Publishing Company, LLC
www.101publishingcompany.com
info@101publishingcompany.com

...I would like to dedicate this book to the one I will always love...

Contents

FOREWORD

On the next one-hundred-plus pages, you will have the opportunity to create a better life for yourself, and most importantly, for your children. The book consists of one hundred and one life-changing principles. Some are very simple; some are more complicated. Read them all and memorize them.

It isn't necessary for you to read this book from the beginning. Start anywhere you want. Keep the book handy and read it every time you lose faith in the path you are taking. Keep it where you can see it; it's small, and it will fit into your backpack, your purse or even your back pocket.

Read this book as many times as possible, or until it becomes second nature to you.

At the end of the book, you will notice an email address. I am hoping that you will write your own story describing how this book changed your life and send it to me. The best stories, with your permission, will be published in Volume II. of this book. I bet you never thought you would become a writer, did you? Well, as you see, life is full of possibilities.

Share this book with your children or ask them to read it alone. It is written so that even twelve-year-old children can understand it. The sooner they know these principles, the better.

Of course, I would like this book to become a bestseller, but this is not why I wrote it. I wrote it because I realized that most of us would read a book like this after we had become adults and would learn so much from it. Can you imagine what your life would be like if you had had this knowledge when you were fourteen or fifteen years old?

My intent was to write this book in a simple form and in simple language so even the youngest reader would be able to understand it and learn from it.

I wish for a better world with less unhappiness and a brighter future for our children and us.

Enjoy reading! This book will change your life, as well as your children's lives!

...You are just one page away from creating a better world...

...One quote and one piece of advice I would like you to remember...

"SHOOT FOR THE MOON. EVEN IF YOU MISS,
YOU'LL LAND AMONG THE STARS."
- NORMAN VINCENT PEALE

...ALIGN YOURSELF WITH THE PRINCIPLES OF
PEACE, LOVE, HARMONY, HEALTH AND JOY AND
GOOD THINGS WILL START HAPPENING
IN YOUR LIFE...

...Just a thought...

A little girl is walking along a beach by the blue ocean and sees thousands of starfish, which have been washed ashore and are dying. She stops to pick up as many as she can and throws them back into the ocean. An old man is passing by and says to her, "Why are you doing that? It's not going to make a difference; there are thousands." The little girl looks at him with her lovely brown eyes and innocent face and says, "If I can make a difference in one of their lives, then it is worth it."

PROTECT THE WEAKER

The human race is so beautiful and so diverse. We are all equal, but we are not all the same. Some of us are tall, some small, some strong and some weak.

Unfortunately, in today's world, we are often taught to aggressively go after anything we want, not to concern ourselves with others and to never look back. We are often told, if you do not take what you want, someone else will.

This path may be impossible for someone who is weak - physically or mentally. Some of us may not be able to easily accomplish our goals or live our lives to the fullest. When this happens, someone stronger must step in and help.

Never make fun of the weak; be there for them even if others look down on them. Show them respect, and offer your help. Your kindness will always come back to you tenfold.

RESPECT THE ELDERS

When we are born, our lives are like a blank canvas. The older we get, the more wisdom, experience and skills we gain and the more colorful the painting on the canvas becomes. It is often our elders who help us grow wiser, guide us toward fulfilling experiences and encourage us to hone our skills.

When you take a moment to think of your grandparents, you likely feel respect and love for them. So, why would you treat other elders with disrespect?

We all can learn from our elders. We will eventually face the same kinds of situations they have faced. Let's try to learn from the ones who are more mature than we are, and let's show them our respect and gratitude. We will one day reach the age they are now, and we will probably not enjoy being disrespected or made fun of.

In human history, the elders have always been the most respected ones.

There is a reason why you have not seen a twenty-year-old president.

LOVE AND RESPECT ANNIMALS

The animal kingdom is full of beautiful creatures. Like humans, they are living beings. They, too, have their own souls, lives and families. They can feel happiness, love, pain and heartache.

Unfortunately, there are people who mistreat and abuse them. They do it from a lack of knowledge, compassion, love and care in their own lives.

Animals bring so much joy into our lives, so return them the kindness. Protect them and treat all of them with love and care.

FOLLOW YOUR DREAMS AND NEVER GIVE UP

Believe me, you can live your dream!

People have so many dreams when they are young. The sky is the limit. As they grow older, they may slowly start giving up on their dreams, settling for less than they had imagined. So, where is the problem?

Other things in life can easily distract people. Sometimes, it is just easier to give up than to continue working hard.

Dreams should always be connected to specific goals: daily, weekly, monthly, and yearly. Dreams without goals are just empty thoughts. Goals must be set in a way that will eventually lead to the fulfillment of your dreams. You will have to learn patience and discipline and accept the fact that failure is often a necessary part of accomplishing your goals. Multiple failures may lead you to think that your dreams make no sense, but if you do not give up on them, and remain faithful, you will eventually succeed. Believe me, you will succeed!

The difference between those who make it and those who do not is that those who make it understand that failure is part of the journey. They keep pushing until they overcome initial obstacles and finally achieve what they dreamed of.

Be strong and never give up! If you were able to dream your dream, it is already yours. Go after it!

CONNECT WITH NATURE

In the hectic world in which we live today, it is extremely important to connect with nature. The "pollution" of cell phones, Wi-Fi and the Internet is extremely harmful to our minds, souls and bodies.

Find a place where you can be alone; where you do not hear any artificial noise. Forget about your cell phone for a while. Instead, look at the greenery, listen to the birds, watch the deer feeding in a meadow, feel the grass with your bare feet, hug the trees and look at the blue sky. This natural world is where we came from, and we need to get back to it, at least sometimes.

If you can connect with nature regularly - a couple of times a week - you will soon see positive effects on your mind, soul and body.

ALWAYS RESPECT YOUR PARENTS

There will be times when you disagree with your parents. This is normal, but it should never turn into a serious, long-term issue or a violent situation.

Your parents gave you life, and you should always appreciate them for it. Show them respect and gratitude.

There will be a day when they leave this world and you will be left alone. You will miss them and wish you could do whatever it would take to bring them back, so you could tell them just one more time, "I love you" and "Thank you."

NEVER CHEAT ANYONE OR STEAL FROM ANYONE

Let me start with this: If you cheat or steal, the hurt you cause will come back to you in the form of lost income, bad health, a lost job, difficulty sleeping, unhappiness or another form that will take something away from you.

Educated, sophisticated, ethical people do not cheat or steal. They do not want to hurt anyone in such a way.

You should know that the world always maintains its equilibrium. If you knowingly take something that does not belong to you, you will eventually pay for it in some form. It might not be right away, but it is guaranteed to happen.

On the other hand, if you give, you will receive tenfold. Keep in mind that giving or taking away doesn't always have to be related to money or material things.

STAY POSITIVE

It would not be fair if I said this one was easy. I too have days when I feel down, as if nothing is working for me and everyone else has it better or easier.

On these days, it is extremely important to think about what you do have, rather than what you do not have. Focus on what you have accomplished, be thankful that you are healthy and be happy for your children, parents, spouse, friends and your pets. Think about something that brings a smile back to your face and excitement to your day. Remember, the sun will rise again tomorrow. A new day will always bring new opportunities.

You need to have a strong will and constantly reject any negative thoughts that come to your mind. When they come, ignore them, erase them and think about something positive.

Create a list of things that always make you happy and turn to them every time negative thoughts try to conquer your mind.

BELIEVE IN A HIGHER POWER

Have you noticed that under certain circumstances, for example when you really wish for something or are facing a difficult situation, you begin to pray or turn to someone or something to ask for help? This may be God, the Universe, or a Guardian Angel.

It is very important to believe in something more powerful than we are. Someone or something created our life, and this someone or something is always there for us. Wherever we go, it is with us, looking after us.

In order to receive a blessing from a higher power, you must first recognize its existence, believe in it and appreciate the blessings you have already received. This higher power is all around us, always ready to help. Recognize it and start believing. You will soon be guided to a better you and a more joyful, successful life.

Remember, you are never alone.

DO NOT STOP EDUCATING YOURSELF

Most of us stop educating ourselves as soon as we finish high school or college.

We learn so much during the years we attend school, but then we find a job, start a family and stop learning new things.

Imagine if you continued studying for the rest of your life. We all would be doctors, scientists, space engineers and who knows what else.

Keep in mind that learning does not require going to school. Just pick a subject in which you are interested, buy books and read about it and study it. Learn to speak a new language, perfect a new skill or learn to play a musical instrument. Your life will become richer and more fulfilling.

ENJOY LIFE; GO AND SMELL THE ROSES

When was the last time you smelled a rose? Today, we do not even have to leave our homes to buy groceries, shop, work or socialize. We can do it all from the comfort of our home. There are so many great benefits from using technology, the Internet and social media! Or, are there?

Nothing will ever replace real touch, smell, sight or sound. Some young people of the current generation, and even some of their parents, have never smelled a rose. They do not know how apples grow. Some of us have started feeling uncomfortable about meeting people, talking to them in person and having fun with them. What have we become?

Do not spend all your free time on the Internet or social media. Go out, enjoy some fresh air, look at the blue sky, listen to birds chirping and smell the flowers all around you.

Appreciate the beauty of life.

FOOD IS OUR LIFE; YOU ARE WHAT YOU EAT

I strongly believe that nutrition and healthy eating habits should be subjects taught in every high school. Unfortunately, social media and TV commercials have taken over and now dictate what is good and healthy to consume. Do not fall for it! If you do, it will catch up to you, and when it does, it may be too difficult to fix.

When I look at others, and without being judgmental, I can tell you who eats what just by looking at their bodies and taking in their overall appearance. There are, of course, exceptions to this; some people have a medical condition that prevents them from being fit and healthy. But no medical condition prevents a person from eating healthy. Soda, fast food and processed food may be convenient, but they should never become a part of our regular diet. It is fine to have a cheat day occasionally, but not every day.

Arguments about not having time to cook, or money to buy healthy foods, are only excuses. Spend less time online and use this time to cook dinner for your family. Involve your children. I am sure they will enjoy learning how to cook; plus, when they grow up, they will be able to teach their kids. Cooking together is a great way to spend quality time with your family.

And the money issue? Well, let's do some math: At a fast food restaurant, for a family of four, you will spend at least fifteen to twenty-five dollars (or more). If you think you cannot prepare a healthy dinner for about the same amount or less, it may be a good idea to visit your local grocery store…soon!

REMEMBER YOUR GRANDPARENTS

We have talked about the principle of respecting the elders in Chapter 2 and your parents in Chapter 6. Respecting your grandparents, who may be the most significant elders in your life, is obviously just as important.

One thing I notice when I travel outside the United States is that children in Europe, Africa and Asia have a close and very respectful relationship with their grandparents. Grandparents gave life to our parents, who then gave life to us. When is the last time you saw your grandfather or your grandmother?

Make some time and pay them a visit, tell them how much you love them and listen to them very carefully when they try to advise you. They have lived a long time; they have been there and done it. Some of the things they say may sound funny now, but you will understand them one day, when you grow older.

Your grandparents have wisdom and life experience, and they are offering it free of charge. So, take advantage of their insight, and while you are with them, tell them how much they mean to you. They will remember your words forever.

TEACH YOUR KIDS WHAT YOU LEARNED
FROM YOUR PARENTS AND GRANDPARENTS

You should try to pass on knowledge and the wisdom gained from experience from one generation to the next. Become a good listener and carefully think about what your parents and grandparents tell you. I guarantee that it will one day pay off big time, especially when you apply this wisdom in your early years.

Preserve your family heritage. Make sure your kids know where your family comes from. Tell them about the struggles your family has had to overcome and the victories they have celebrated. It will help build your children's character and establish respect for your family.

Knowing your family's history, and keeping the lessons in mind that you've learned from your parents and grandparents, may help you to overcome personal, family or business-related issues down the road.

FIND TIME TO THANK GOD OR A HIGHER POWER

In Chapter 9, **Believe in a Higher Power**, I explained why it was important to believe in someone or something bigger than ourselves.

When we accomplish something, we know that it took time, effort and hard work. But we should never forget that it also took someone or something besides us to help us arrive at our desired destination. We should always show our gratitude and thanks for what was made possible.

If you show your appreciation for what you have, you will get more of it.

Look at some of the most successful people in the world. They all will tell you, or at least the wise ones will, that they must thank God for what was made possible. So, take some time during your day and give thanks for what you have and what you will have.

DO NOT WORRY; EVERYTHING WILL EVENTUALLY WORK OUT

There are times when we work on something, try really hard and spend a lot of time and energy to accomplish our goal(s), but it does not work. We get frustrated, angry and demotivated.

Well, I have learned that if you did your very best and it still did not work out, then it was probably not meant to be. This shouldn't mean, under any circumstances, you need to give up after the first few failures.

Sometimes failures can redirect our life journey somewhere that is even more exciting than we had imagined. Trust me; this is usually the case.

There is an old saying: Nothing is bad without being good for something.

SHOW PEOPLE LOVE AND CARE

Can you describe the way you feel when your parents, spouse, friends or someone else shows you love and care? You probably feel very comfortable, secure, happy, special and appreciated.

Please note that when we talk about expressing love, it does not have to be connected to an intimate relationship. You can show your love and care to anyone. This act will make you feel good and will never go unnoticed by others.

Remember, people who give, not only in terms of money or material gifts, will be rewarded tenfold.

Some examples of love include holding hands with your spouse, doing chores someone else does not like, giving your time, doing little things like opening a door for someone, letting someone go in front of you in a line or anything that would make someone feel appreciated and cared for.

We never know what is on someone's mind. Sometimes, small acts of kindness can make a huge difference, and maybe even save a life.

HELP THE LESS FORTUNATE

Some of us, when we were little, had the pleasure of having a pet: a puppy, kitten or maybe something else. Do you remember when you went to the pet store to choose your fluffy best friend? You probably saw several adorable furry balls, all full of life and energy and excited to see you. You knew you wanted the best and strongest one.

But then you noticed something small in a corner, shaking and watching you, wishing you would pick him even though he was the weakest one and you probably wouldn't like him. Or so he thought. Your heart melted and you picked him and promised to take care of him as best you could. As payback, he grew stronger and even cuter and loved you with all his heart, forever and unconditionally.

The same applies to humans. We should never forget about the less fortunate among us, whether their handicap is caused by their health, the way they look, the way they live or something else that makes them different.

The less fortunate always need some extra love, care and attention.

DO NOT BE RUDE; YOU WILL HURT SOMEONE

There are days when we do not feel exactly great. We all have them. On those days, we may want everyone around us to feel as we do.

In a situation like this, we need to remember that we are not functioning properly; the chemistry in our brain is simply "off," and we do not realize what consequences our behavior could have.

Leaving extremes, such as abusive or violent physical behavior, aside, most of us will become verbally offensive. We may say things that we really do not mean. But those things, once said, will hurt someone.

Some people are more sensitive than others, and your rude comments can be more than they can ignore. People around us have their own problems and stresses. They may be dealing with a sad situation, family or other difficult issue, and your comments could make them feel even worse.

When we feel we are having one of our not-so-great days, the best thing to do is to avoid commenting on or arguing with others so you do not say something you will regret later. And if you cannot control yourself, just walk away.

WHEN YOU MAKE IT, REACH BACK AND HELP OTHERS

When you become successful (not if, but when), help someone else reach their dreams.

Your help does not have to be in the form of money. It can be the time you spend sharing your own experiences and advising or mentoring others. Become living proof that dreams really do come true.

SHOWING YOUR EMOTIONS IS NOT A SIGN OF WEAKNESS

This topic will probably relate more to men than to women. The trend now is to always look strong and suppress one's emotions. Expressing our emotions is often seen as a sign of weakness, but this could not be further from the truth.

Expressing emotions can help release stress, and therefore it helps your mind, soul and body. It also allows you to identify and resolve any issue quicker.

Expressing genuine feelings brings people closer together and creates stronger relationships.

So, the next time you feel emotional about something, do not be afraid to shed a tear or ask for a hug. You will immediately feel much better.

ANGER NEVER SOLVES ANYTHING; THE PRINCIPLE OF FF

During our lives, we will face many situations that could make us angry. Things will seem to be unfair, and we will naturally try to fight them. Before I learned about the Principle of FF, a simple unpleasant experience could trigger my anger, spoil my whole day and make people around me miserable.

The Principle of FF means Forgive and Forget. It can be applied in any situation. It will lead to immediate relief and an improvement in your outlook.

So, the next time something or someone makes you angry, forgive the person involved, forget about what happened and simply move on with your day. You will be much happier.

ALWAYS TREAT WOMEN WITH LOVE AND RESPECT

Think of women as if they were beautiful flowers. They are fragile, elegant and beautiful and must be protected and treated with love, care and respect.

As much as I believe in equality between men and women, I also realize that Mother Nature has made a woman's role in this world different than the role of a man.

All women - our mothers, wives, sisters, girlfriends and friends - must be looked up to and pampered. Please remember this and never forget that every woman really is a blessing.

VIOLANCE IS NOT A SOLUTION TO ANYTHING

Violent acts have never solved anything. They only bring more sorrow, sadness and unhappiness to our lives. They cause misery that can last a lifetime.

Aggressors who commit violent acts will be reminded of them constantly throughout life. Such behavior can eventually lead to the destruction of the aggressor's own soul.

I wish that one day we would be able to erase all violence from this world. I know that with your help, we can do so and make this world a peaceful place where we all can live together, regardless of our skin color, origin or religion.

IF YOU CAN, DONATE YOUR TIME AND MONEY TO A GOOD CAUSE

Anyone anywhere at any time can donate time or money. We do not have to be famous or millionaires to do it. In fact, it should become a way of life.

You can start donating a little bit every year, and then, if you want to and are able to, you can increase the frequency.

Remember that the amount of money or time you donate is not important, but the act of doing it and your good intentions are.

DO NOT LOOK DOWN ON ANYONE

Whether or not you think you have a reason to look down on someone, doing so is always very impolite, selfish, hurtful and a sign of an immature personality.

If you are tempted to look down on someone, think about what is compelling you to do so. Is there something you can do that will cause you to think in a different, more positive way? If there is something that can be done, do it. If not, accept people the way they are; respect them and move on.

LAUGHTER, FUN AND JOY WILL HEAL AND SOLVE ANY PROBLEM

People who have fun, are joyful and laugh often are happier, healthier and more attractive. When you laugh and have fun, your body releases endorphins, a natural chemical. Endorphins have a positive effect on your body by boosting your heart rate and producing certain antibodies that help your immune system.

Sometimes, we take life too seriously. But if we can manage to have fun and enjoy every moment possible, the problems we deal with will often seem less complicated and easier to resolve.

So, if you want to live a happy, long life, be successful, have good health and good looks, try to laugh, have fun and enjoy everything you do.

YOUR FAMILY IS EVERYTHING

Why is your family so important? Because they have been there for you from the very beginning, since you were born, and they will be there when you die - because they love you unconditionally.

It is your family who helps you during difficult times. Your family is a peaceful place you can always turn to. They will always be there for you. So, do not ever take them for granted. Instead, tell them how much you love them today, tomorrow and every day thereafter.

BE OPEN-MINDED

Being open-minded was always difficult for me, and I look up to those who have that ability.

Most of us accept a set of beliefs and values during our lives. We then try to adhere to them every time we encounter a situation that presents us with more options.

There is nothing wrong with having strong opinions or views about a specific topic, but sometimes accepting new ideas and opinions and trying new things can be very rewarding.

Try to be open-minded! Your life will become richer!

60

TRAVEL OUT OF THE COUNTRY BY THE TIME YOU ARE TWENTY-ONE

When I was a teenager, my parents would travel out of the country and take my brother and me with them. Yes, we were very fortunate. We were not rich, but somehow our parents always managed to travel. Believe it or not, almost forty years later, I still remember our trips as if they were yesterday. By the age of sixteen, I had visited seven countries and enjoyed their local cuisines, colorful cultures, fascinating people and any adventures that came with it.

I learned new things, and I became more open-minded and perhaps more sophisticated. I am still very grateful for those opportunities, and even now, every time I have a chance to travel, I do.

I urge you to take a trip. You do not have to spend a fortune. Explore new cultures and new places, meet nice people and taste different foods. The sooner you can do this, the better!

Traveling was, and still is, one of the best moments in my life. I would like you to try it, too. You will see that it will make a difference in your life, as well.

DO NOT ALWAYS BELIEVE WHAT YOU SEE ON THE NEWS

In today's world, it is easy for our minds to be influenced by outside forces.

From the moment we turn on the morning news, throughout the day as we surf the Internet and check our social media websites, to evening when we sit down in front of the TV, people are trying to tell us their stories, offer their opinions, give us their advice, predict the future or show off their latest achievements. Should you always believe everything they tell you? My advice to you is: No!

Stay open-minded, verify the facts, be curious, think about the purpose of a message, reach your own conclusions and ask questions. But, most importantly, live your own life.

NEVER COMMIT A CRIME; IT WILL ALWAYS CATCH UP WITH YOU

Let me remind you about what we learned in Chapter 7, **Never Cheat Anyone or Steal from Anyone**. The world in which we live maintains its own equilibrium, and committing a crime will upset the balance.

By committing a crime, you not only hurt the one you victimize, but you hurt yourself, as well. The punishment might not come right away, but it is sure to come, and probably when you expect it the least.

The invisible powers will come upon you and force you to bring the world back into balance. You took something from someone, and now you will need to give back for causing distress. The giving will be in the form of lost happiness, insomnia, money losses, embarrassment, jail time, regrets or any other way that makes you suffer.

NEVER CHEAT ON YOUR SPOUSE

If you do cheat on your spouse, your relationship will never be the same.

When two people decide to get married, they promise to stay faithful to each other for the rest of their lives. When one of them breaks this promise, it is the beginning of a long and unhappy period of their life.

If you are tempted to break your promise, run away (literally) from the source of temptation. The short-term pleasure is never worth the long-term pain you will cause to your partner and to yourself.

RESOLVE ALL ARGUMENTS BEFORE BEDTIME

This should be easy, but it will require a commitment from you.

This principle does not apply only to husband-and-wife relationships. Arguments with any person in your life should be resolved as soon as possible, and definitely before you go to sleep. If you drag a problem to the next day, it will cause even more harm and pain than it already has.

Start each new day with a clean slate, with no troubling issues on your mind or in your heart. The best way to do this is to forgive and forget and kiss and hug each other before you go to sleep. This way, you can welcome the new day with excitement and expectations of only the best.

DO NOT CRITICIZE OR JUDGE; RESPECT OTHERS

All people are equal, regardless of their skin color, origin, religion, age or any other attribute that could make them look, think, act or feel differently than you.

It is normal not to like everyone, but it is not normal to criticize or judge a person for being different than you.

Every time you are tempted to criticize or judge, think of how it would feel if you were the one who was the object of criticism or judgment. I am sure you would not like it. So, why would you do it to someone else?

Show everyone respect by accepting them just the way they are.

BE PATIENT AND DO NOT GIVE UP WHEN YOU ENCOUNTER A FIRST OBSTACLE

You have probably heard stories from successful businessmen or sportsmen and famous actors or singers about their journeys as they followed their dreams. They all have one thing in common: Success was never handed to them; they had to earn it. They had to work very hard to get where they are now, and they nearly always had to overcome multiple failures and setbacks.

One thing they did not do was give up when chasing their dream became difficult. They kept going and were patient, believing that their dream would one day come true. They did not give up!

Oftentimes, giving up is easier than going through struggles. If you manage to keep on going, working hard day after day, you will eventually be rewarded by your dream coming true.

The secret is that everyone could accomplish their dreams if they were patient and never gave up.

Successful people have gained wealth by seeing opportunities where others saw obstacles.

TRY TO MAKE PROGRESS EVERY DAY; SET GOALS

Doing "something" is always more productive than doing "nothing."

I always like to use the example of learning a new language. Just imagine if you decided to learn ten new words every day. It is a task anyone can accomplish. Ten new words a day are three hundred new words a month and a stunning thirty-six hundred new words a year. Even if you managed to do this only every other day, you would still know over *fifteen hundred* words of a new language after a year.

My point is that doing a little on a regular basis will eventually amount to an amazing achievement.

Set goals for yourself for each day, week or month. Aim for a little progress or improvement every day. You will soon enjoy the benefits of doing a little bit on a regular basis.

THE "ONE DAY" NEVER COMES; ACT NOW!

I just turned forty years old. Up until two years ago, I kept saying that "one day" I would do this or that. When will this fabulous "one day" arrive? I am sorry to burst your bubble, but no, "one day" will never come unless you act now!

We have so many ideas and so many dreams, but we often say, "One day I will do this. One day I will do that." You know how quickly time flies, and I guarantee you, you will turn sixty and you will keep saying "one day." So, let me tell you something, and you'd better listen: The "one day" just came, and it is today.

Do the things you want to do now. Do not procrastinate or wait for a better moment than today. Today is the "one day," so start acting on your dreams, goals and plans. **One Day** you will be very happy you started today.

SUCCESS WILL ALWAYS COME; IT JUST DEPENDS ON HOW MUCH YOU WANT IT

In the beginning, it will seem impossible to accomplish what you want. You will have to deal with problems, failures and discouragement, and giving up will seem to be the only rational choice. This is exactly the moment when 99% of people give up, the moment when their dreams remain dreams - empty dreams. But this is also the moment when the 1% decides to continue, no matter what, and finally turns their dreams into a reality.

All successful people had to go through exactly the same experiences. Failure was on their daily schedule, but they pushed through it. For some reason, they wanted to succeed more than others. And they eventually did.

Before you even start with something, decide whether you belong to the 99% or the 1% of fearless life changers. I am sure you belong to the latter. Go chase your dreams and make a difference.

SUCCESS REALLY DOES NOT DEPEND ON YOUR BACKGROUND OR WHERE YOU COME FROM

Rich or poor, black or white, married or divorced; these are often used as excuses to justify a failure.

I have personally known rich families whose children never accomplished anything great. I have seen poor men and women become leaders and successful businesspeople. I have seen both black and white people become rich, as well as poor.

My point is that your life does not have to be influenced by where you come from, who your parents are, the color of your skin or any other characteristic that might come to your mind.

You are the only one who is in full control of your life and destiny. There is no one and nothing that has the right to stop you from getting what you want.

Listen to your heart, and go after what you dream of.

FEAR AND WORRY WILL ONLY HURT YOU

I am sure you have gone through times when you were fearful or worried about something, but after a while, you realized there was actually no reason to worry.

Do not get me wrong; worrying is not bad, but it should not ever take over your mind and control your emotions or actions. Some say that worrying will make you perform better, and I agree with that to a certain point.

If you are facing a difficult situation with an uncertain outcome, do not spend your energy worrying too much, but believe that the invisible powers of the universe, whether it is God or something else you believe in, will always stand by and guide you through difficult situations without harm.

You must remain faithful and believe that everything will eventually be all right.

START WHEN YOU ARE YOUNG

It is never too late to start, but if you manage to start in your early years, when you are still young, full of energy and, most importantly, without any major responsibilities, such as supporting a family, raising children or paying for a mortgage, it will be much easier and less stressful. You will also have a significant head start compared with those who start in their later years. In general, it is just easier to start early.

If you have an idea, work on it now; do not delay. Remember, the "one day" is today.

If you do not manage to start early, believe that it is never too late to start anything at any age. You just need to want it and start working on it!

THE FIRST SEVEN YEARS OF YOUR LIFE

This is intended more for your parents or for you when you become a parent. A person's mind and body absorb the most during the first seven years of life. Every child is like a sponge. This is the time when a person's character and personality are formed and abilities are discovered.

In the first seven years, children should be exposed only to positive things. They should experience new things, they should travel and they should be constantly encouraged, motivated and supported.

The first seven years are like a foundation of a house. If a foundation is built improperly, it will collapse. On the other hand, if it is built from the best materials, using the best techniques, it will withstand even the strongest storm.

Give your kids the best seven years you can. The effort will eventually come back to you in the form of joy and pride at having happy, healthy and successful children.

BE CONSIDERATE OF THE ENVIRONMENT

As you already know, the universe maintains its equilibrium. You have learned more about this in other chapters of this book. The principles of balance apply to our relationship with the environment, as well.

The way you treat the environment will always come back to you. If you treat it with consideration and care for its gifts, you will be repaid with the beauty of nature, pleasing landscapes, an abundance of flowers, trees, animals and health and happiness for yourself and others. If you are careless about the environment and ignore its needs, you will soon find yourself living in a polluted world, fighting impoverishment and disease.

If you do not know how to start, educate yourself. There are many ways you can help the environment. You just need to want to do so and truly care about the world.

DIET, EXERCISE AND EMOTIONAL HEALTH
ARE THE KEYS TO SUCCESS

Most people focus only on their diet, exercise or emotional health - not on all three.

In order to live a happy, healthy and successful life, you need to consider all three equally: exercise and a healthy diet nourish your body, and emotional health nourishes your soul. If you omit one, you will not have the proper balance. Balance is absolutely necessary for you to be healthy, happy and successful. From what I have seen, most people neglect their emotional health.

Take some time to be alone with yourself, meditate, think about what makes you happy and express your gratefulness for who you are and what you have. Become at peace with all and everything.

Only when you pay attention to all three will you achieve happiness, health and success. It is not an accident that they are a set of three.

DO NOT PAY ATTENTION TO WHAT OTHERS SAY ABOUT YOU

No one has the right to judge you or to speak badly about you. If they do, you should not let it consume you.

Every person is different, and each one has different opinions, values and expectations. Each one looks and acts differently, too. Every person is unique, and this is one of the things that makes our world beautiful and endlessly interesting. Be proud of yourself.

If you are always doing your best and are sticking to great values and ethics, you should not pay attention to what others say about you. Of course, some comments might be a form of useful criticism, and when you encounter such a comment, you should be able to determine if it is constructive or not. If it is, learn from it. If it is not, forget about it and move on.

Be yourself; you do not always have to please everyone around you.

Be proud of the way you are.

DO NOT LET BULLYING AFFECT YOUR LIFE

Bullying is unethical and a horrible action conducted by unhappy people who have low self-esteem and no values. Often, those who bully are unloved and misunderstood in their own lives.

When you encounter bullying, the best defense is not to show the person that you are hurt. Be strong and maintain your peaceful state. If you can, avoid being close to those unhappy people and surround yourself with good and positive people.

When you show a bully that you are strong and self-confident, the bullying will often stop. You can use the same approach to help others who find themselves being bullied.

If the bullying does not stop, do not be afraid to tell your parents, friends or other people around you and ask for help. Believe me, it is not a sign of weakness. Asking for help is a sign of wisdom, maturity and a strong personality.

Under no circumstances let bullying affect your life, health or happiness.

WORKING OR STUDYING HARD IS NOTHING TO BE ASHAMED OF

I am sure that during your life, you will hear, at least once, people making fun of you. They will call you a nerd, mommy's boy or girl, party pooper or other insulting name(s). The people making fun of you do not realize that you are actually building a foundation for a successful life.

By working and studying hard, you are pursuing your future goals and dreams.

Believe me, you can get over those few moments when others make fun of you. The pain will fade away very quickly, and you will soon find yourself in a position where people who once made fun of you are addressing you as boss, president or Your Honor.

Study and work as hard as you can. It will always, and I repeat again, *always,* pay off.

YOUR FUTURE WILL BE WHAT YOU
MENTALLY PICTURE IT TO BE

Your mind is a powerful medium. Every time you think about something, you subconsciously create a mental picture. If you focus on this picture long enough, it will eventually become real.

It is important to be extremely careful about what you think. Every thought has the ability to create this mental picture, and your mind will always respond by turning it into a reality, whether good or bad.

Your thoughts should only be positive, and any negative thoughts must be immediately denied and rejected.

DO NOT DWELL ON YOUR PAST

There is no benefit in being caught in the past.

Of course, it is understandable that some feelings or memories can cause us to dwell on something that happened long ago. In these situations, we need to realize that there is nothing we can do to change the past. We simply cannot turn back time, at least not yet.

The best approach is to accept the past for what it is and start enjoying the present and looking forward to what life will bring in the future. It will help not only you, but also the ones around you.

Life is like driving a car: As we drive, we need to pay attention to what is in front of us. This is the reason the windshield in a car is larger than the rear-view mirror - to help us move forward and focus on the road ahead. There are times when we need to look in the rear-view mirror, too, but looking at it all the time would prevent us from moving forward and seeing the road ahead.

WHAT MATTERS IS ALWAYS FREE

If tomorrow never comes, and all you have fades away, what will you have left?

All the fancy things we have - or strive to have - will no longer matter, right? What will really matter is your family and friends and the love and care you have shared with them, so put what really matters first.

The important things will always be there, no matter what. And they will always be there for you for free.

THE BEST INVESTMENT YOU CAN MAKE IS IN YOU

There are many ways to invest your time and money, but there is only one investment that will never lose its value: investing in yourself.

Every time you have an opportunity to learn, or to see or experience something new, go for it.

If you continue to invest in yourself throughout your life, you will continue to receive the many dividends this wise investment will yield.

Anything enriching your life can be considered an investment in yourself; for example, learning a new language, reading about a new subject, perfecting new skills, traveling to a new place or gaining a new experience.

When you invest in yourself, the benefits will stay with you forever. No one will ever be able to take them away from you.

YOU CAN ALWAYS MAKE MORE MONEY, BUT YOU CANNOT MAKE MORE TIME

You should be happy to learn this now, hopefully early in your life. Most people, including myself, realize this when it is almost too late.

Money is important, very important, but it is never more important than the time you spend with your family and friends.

Time is something you can only spend. You will never be able to save it. We are all living on borrowed time, so use it wisely.

BUT I HAVE A HANDICAP

Great, so now turn the handicap into an advantage.

Living with a handicap is not easy, but you are proving, every day, that you have what it takes to be successful.

Most people who face some kind of obstacle or barrier, whether it is physical, emotional or anything else, are stronger than the ones without the handicap.

Do not let this handicap limit you and control your life. Do what you have dreamed of doing. Do not be afraid. I guarantee that you will be more successful than others.

You may have been born with a challenge, but you were also born with attributes that others might lack, such as determination, patience and a strong desire to succeed. So, use them to your advantage.

YOU WILL BECOME WHAT YOU ENVISION YOURSELF TO BE

I am living proof that what you envision and believe in will eventually come true. It is difficult to explain, but it works. It has worked for me, and it will work for you, too. Your vision is your future.

The vision, however, must be combined with a true desire to get where you want to be in life. If you add hard work and patience, it is almost impossible to fail.

The vision is like the seed that is planted and later develops into a beautiful flower or a tree. Have a vision…a clear vision. The greater the vision, the richer your life will be.

Just remember, nothing is for free, and therefore your vision must always be supported by your true desire and willingness to work hard for what you want.

BE CAREFUL ABOUT WHAT YOU THINK OF OTHERS

We mentioned in another chapter that your mind and thoughts are powerful and can turn every mental picture you subconsciously create into reality.

Just as the picture of yourself that you paint in your mind is based on faith, belief and an expectation of all the best, the picture you create in your mind of others will also eventually become a reality.

If you think ill of others, the picture of them in your mind can also eventually become a reality in some way.

Rather than thinking of people in a negative way, try to always find something positive about them. You will find that this will change the way you see others and perhaps also provide for an opportunity to improve your relationship with them.

HAVING NEGATIVE THOUGHTS? ERASE THEM IMMEDIATELY!

This will require some time. You will have to train yourself to deal with negative thoughts. Eventually, you will get to the point where you pay them no attention.

When you have negative thoughts, picture an imaginary wall that has the power to block all bad thoughts. This is what I do every time a negative thought tries to attack my mind. I simply do not let it in. I quickly reject it, deny it and start focusing on something nice and positive.

Dwelling on negative thoughts will not do any good. Do not waste your time on it. Have a list nearby of things that always make you happy, and every time you are tempted to waste your time on negative thoughts, read your list and quickly turn your attention to something positive.

DISCRIMINATION AND RACISM

Black or white, Christian or Muslim, young or old, man or woman - none of these descriptions make any difference. We all have blood flowing in our veins, breathe the same air and are born from our mothers. The world is beautiful because it is so diverse.

Being a racist, or discriminating against others, is a sign of weakness, a lack of education and life experience.

No person, race or religion should ever supersede others. We are all equal and beautiful exactly the way we are.

Being able to respect differences among humans is a sign of wisdom and sophistication. When you genuinely love and care about others, you will see no differences among them. If we were all the same, our world would become a boring place in which to live.

Enjoy the beauty and appreciate the diversity.

DO NOT ENVY OR BE JEALOUS

Envy and jealousy will never get you anywhere. If anything, they will cause you to suffer and develop health issues. Envy and jealousy should have absolutely no place in your life.

If there is something you do not have but someone else does, use it as motivation and proof that dreams really can come true. Be happy for others, what they have and what they have accomplished. The way you act toward others will eventually come back to you.

I have many times wished I could have what others have, but I never feel envious or jealous. Instead, I try to find a way to accomplish the same.

When someone else has something I wish for, I use it as an incentive and inspiration. I am always happy for that person. I know that if I really want something, I can have it, too.

YOU CAN PROGRAM YOUR MIND

People do not realize that we are all in full control of our minds. When you decide to run, you run. You simply order your mind to get your body in motion. You do not think about it; you do not question it. It comes naturally, and you do not expect anything other than that you are going to run. The same principle applies to anything you ask your mind to execute.

Tonight, when you go sleep, do not turn on your alarm, but instead tell your mind clearly - without a doubt - what time you will wake up. Before you fall asleep, repeat this to yourself several times: I will wake up at 7:00 a.m. (or whenever you wish to wake up). Then, fall asleep, confident that you will wake up at exactly 7:00 a.m.

You will see that you will wake up at 7:00 a.m. the next morning. This is only simple evidence that you really can program your mind to do just about anything.

ALWAYS BE HUMBLE AND KIND

Some people, when they become wealthy, turn into arrogant, self-centered individuals. Most are people who did not have to work hard for what they now have. They may have won the lottery, inherited a fortune or gotten their money dishonestly.

Because their wealth came quickly, they skipped the most important part of the journey: learning how to be patient, make sacrifices and appreciate what they have or have accomplished.

When you become wealthy, famous or successful, do not ever forget how it was when you did not have all the fame, wealth and attention. Never take it for granted, and never look down on someone just because they have less than you.

Stay humble and kind. If you can, help others accomplish as much as you have. Become a blessing in someone else's life, not a thorn in their side.

BE SMART WITH YOUR MONEY

Easy come; easy go. This applies especially to money. When you have money, be extremely careful about how you spend it. When you do not have money...well...be extremely careful how you spend it, too. Why? Because loans and credit cards are readily available, and banks and credit institutions compete for your business.

Loans and credit cards may seem like quick and easy ways to satisfy your needs, wishes and desires, but they can quickly turn against you and leave you with a growing debt that will affect you for many years. In some situations, you could face the consequences for the rest of your life.

Before you buy anything, ask yourself whether or not you really need it and whether or not you can actually afford it. If you must get a loan or use your credit card, then I suggest that you wait; you cannot afford it just yet. There is nothing wrong with not being able to afford it. The right time will eventually come.

My advice to you is, if you have any savings, spend it wisely. If you do not, think twice before taking out a loan or using a credit card. Remember that making money is always very difficult, so spend your money wisely.

95

LIVE YOUR LIFE AS IF TOMORROW WILL NOT COME

If you knew today was your last day, what would you do? With whom would you spend your day? Where would you go?

Well, I am sure you can answer these questions. You know the answers, so act accordingly.

When people are dying, they never regret what they did, unless it was something bad, but they always regret what they did not do. Believe me, having regrets when you grow old is most people's worst nightmare.

Start living your life as if today is your last day. If you do, you will never have to worry about having regrets later in life.

98

THE MOST PRECIOUS THING WE ALL HAVE IS TIME

No one has ever figured out how to make more time. And no one will ever figure this out. Never.

The amount of time we are given is fixed. Some of us will have more time, some will have less. But all of us will eventually run out of time.

You cannot make more time, so spend it the best way possible.

IT IS THE WISER ONE WHO RETREATS

It is not a shameful act to retreat, especially if it can avoid a serious argument or a violent act. We do not always have to be right, prove our point or have the last word.

Sometimes, retreating actually means winning. You may not realize your victory right away, but it will eventually become clear. When that happens, you will be proud that you made a wiser decision.

RESPECT OTHER PEOPLE'S PROPERTY

You should always treat other people's property the same as you treat your own.

When people own something, they take good care of it (at least most of them). They probably had to work hard for it. They are happy to have it and want to enjoy it for a long time. I usually say that you should treat the property of others even better than your own.

Imagine how you would feel if someone mistreated the items you like or love. You would feel angry and hurt. So, show your respect and always care, with great concern, for things that do not belong to you.

GET READY; THERE WILL BE FAILURES IN YOUR LIFE

Life happens. Life is beautiful, but it can sometimes be overwhelming or disappointing.

You have to accept the fact that it will not always be perfect and that there will be failures. When failures occur, it is important not to give up or let the disappointment spoil your joy and excitement. Don't allow the failures to divert you from your life goals and dreams.

Remember that failures usually lead to something greater, something that would not have been possible if the failures hadn't occurred first.

Failures are sometimes necessary to reach our goals and dreams.

READING BOOKS IS SPECIAL; TRY IT!

Reading books is different than reading articles on the Internet, your computer or your tablet. A book has its own soul, and the more you read, the more you realize this.

While you are reading a book, you cannot also be doing something else. It takes all of your attention.

When you read a book, you are in a world that contains only you and the book. Your mind can devote your full attention to the subject about which you are reading, and therefore you get more out of it. Try it and you will see; flip through the pages of a book, feel the cover and inhale the unique scent only books have.

Reading a book is, simply, a very special treat.

THE REAL JOY IS IN HELPING OTHERS, NOT IN THINGS WITH WHICH WE SURROUND OURSELVES

Sure, we are happy for the things we have. We use them, enjoy them and show them off. They make us feel fulfilled in some ways.

But have you tried helping others; maybe buying something that a person could not afford on their own, or helping a person in some other way?

You will see that the joy and feeling you receive from doing something for others is much stronger, more fulfilling and more satisfying than just making yourself happy by surrounding yourself with material objects.

Give and you will be given.

TRUE DESIRE IN YOUR HEART IS GOD'S INDICATION THAT SOMETHING IS ALREADY YOURS

Everyone wants something. But there is a significant difference between wanting and desiring.

A desire is like a fire inside you that does not allow you to sleep, rest or stop thinking about what you want. It makes you excited; your heartbeat increases every time you talk about it; you smile when you think about it and you know there is no one and nothing that can stop you from getting it.

You are willing to sacrifice and work tirelessly; failures do not mean anything to you except as a sign that you are getting closer to achieving your dreams. This is true desire. It has nothing in common with wanting.

When you have this true desire, something magical happens. The entire world, the universe, the stars, the higher power or something or someone else we do not know about yet will recognize the force and desire you have lit up inside you. The powers of the universe will go to work and do their part to help you get to your desired destination.

True desire causes miracles. When you start feeling the fire inside you, do not ever let it die.

ASPIRE TO MAKE A DIFFERENCE, NOT JUST A LIVING

Most people do their best to make a living, take care of their family, provide for their kids and pay their bills. They continue doing this until the end of their lives.

There are also those who do all of that and more: they aspire to make a difference. These are the people you hear about on TV, read about in books or newspapers and learn about in school.

You can ask, how were they able to do it? Did they have something I did not have? No, they did not have more than you. But what they had was an aspiration to make a difference. To be remembered.

You can become one of them. Do not ever settle for less; do not just make a living. Aspire to change the world to make it a better place!

WILL YOU HAVE REGRETS WHEN YOUR TIME COMES?

From time to time, it is important to reflect on your life: what you have accomplished, what you have experienced, where you are now and where you eventually want to be.

This will help you realize whether you are meeting your life goals and are happy. If you find out that all is going according to your expectations, then simply continue doing what you are doing.

If you conclude that you missed something somewhere during your life journey, do not get frustrated, but make adjustments, set new goals and go in a new direction.

The worst thing you can do is to ignore the fact that you are not living your life to its full potential and up to your expectations.

Remember that when your time comes, you will never regret the things you did; you will only regret the things you did not do.

GO OUT AND MEET PEOPLE

Before cell phones and the Internet were invented, people had to physically meet if they wanted to get together.

Now, technology has made it possible for us to "get together" without even leaving our living rooms. Virtual meetings on social media have replaced actual physical meetings.

Yes, it is very convenient, but only to a certain point. You should never allow technology to replace genuine interactions. Meeting someone in person is so much more fun, interesting and rewarding. You use all your senses; you practice and improve your interpersonal skills. This will eventually help you with your family, career, business and any other aspect of your life.

If you have an opportunity to see someone, always go for the real deal: meet in person.

PLANT A TREE OR FLOWER

Planting something may be one of the many ways you can help the environment.

If you have a yard, plant a tree; if you do not, at least plant a flower in a pot. Either way, you will be rewarded with the natural beauty and delicious scent of the blossoms. If you want to please your taste buds, why not plant a fruit tree? You will not be able to wait for it to start bearing fruit. Believe me, you will love eating your own organic cherries, plums, apples or whatever it may be.

Just make sure to supply plenty of love, care, sunshine and water.

LEARN TO LOVE YOURSELF

We love other people, our family, children, spouse and our friends. We care about them and always do our best to make sure they are happy, healthy and doing great. This is how it should be. Do not forget to include yourself among those you care about, and this includes your body, your mind and your soul.

You need to give yourself the same attention you give others. There is nothing wrong with making yourself happy, pleasing your senses and nourishing your body, mind and soul.

Pamper yourself, rest, relax and enjoy. Remember, in order to love others, you first need to know how to love yourself.

THERE IS A SOLUTION TO EVERY PROBLEM

I am sure you have been through many situations when you had to deal with a problem. I know that most of those problems, if not all, were resolved, usually in a way that was acceptable for you.

Just as there is an answer to every question, there is a solution to every problem. Sometimes, we worry too much about a problem, only to later find that there was no reason to worry.

I have learned that if you always do your very best, any problem will be resolved to your satisfaction. It can seem, at first, that the outcome is not exactly what you expected, but you will understand it later. Usually, you will be happy with the results.

Have faith and worry less. Every problem will get resolved in a way that eventually is the best resolution for you.

IT IS NEVER TOO LATE TO START

What is great about life is the fact that you can do anything, and you can start doing it at any time. Unfortunately, most people have a mental block about this. They believe that after reaching a certain age, they have missed the opportunity to start something great. This could not be further from the truth.

Sometimes, starting at a later age is better than starting at an earlier age, and vice versa. Your age should never limit you or discourage you from what you would like to do.

If you have an idea or a desire, it is already an indication - a proof - that you should act on it. Look around: There have been people old and young who have had an idea and started working on it, regardless of their age, and become successful.

Your age is just a number. Do not let this number control your life.

THE GRASS IS NEVER GREENER ON THE OTHER SIDE OF THE FENCE

Sometimes, when you look around, you see people who seem to be happy, healthy and successful. They seem to have it all, while you are dealing with regular day-to-day issues. You get frustrated and wonder how it is possible that they are doing so much better than you.

Never forget that when people are outside, they leave their issues inside. All you see is what they want you to see. No one will show off their financial problems, relationship problems or health issues.

Believe me that regardless of how it seems, we all have to deal with the same struggles. If you were able to see inside the lives of other people, you would very soon discover that you are not actually doing that badly.

Really, the grass is never greener on the other side of the fence.

117

LISTEN TO YOUR HEART

Your heart will always be honest with you. Its voice may be quiet sometimes, but it can be very loud, too.

Your mind, on the other hand, will usually lead you to a rational decision. But your heart really does not care whether the decision is rational or the best choice of all. Your heart will always take into account your higher purpose and also your true desires.

Decisions made by your heart might not present the best-case scenario for you, but they are usually the best decisions and you will remember them forever.

Decisions made by listening to your heart are decisions that make a difference in your life, or even better, in someone else's life. A very satisfying feeling that you have done something very, very special will always follow decisions made by your heart.

LISTEN TO YOUR BODY

Working hard, whether at work, at home (taking care of your family and household), in the gym or somewhere else, is great, but we should not continue without proper rest.

Our bodies have a safety feature built in that lets us know when it is time to rest and when it is time to take action. Perhaps I should add that this feature works well only if we pay attention to it.

I am a workaholic; I always try to do my best at home, at work and in the gym. I have noticed that if I continue without rest for a long time, my body always lets me know that it is time to slow down. If I do not listen to its message, it will eventually force me to stop and recover. When this happens, I usually end up at home sick for a few days. I still tend to ignore my body's requests for rest, but I have gotten better at listening. Now I know that when I start feeling tired, exhausted or overwhelmed, I need to slow down.

Listen to your body; it will prevent you from getting sick and from having to deal with other health-related issues.

STAY ACTIVE AND EXERCISE

People who stay active and exercise live longer, look younger, feel more confident and are more successful. Do you need another reason to start?

In order to be active, we do not have to become professional athletes, but we do need to get up and move. Today's hectic lifestyle, which causes us to have to split our energy between our home and work life, does not leave us enough time for exercise.

You need to make an "executive decision" and incorporate exercise into your life. You will be doing it for yourself, as well as for your family. Believe me, you all will enjoy its benefits.

By exercise, I do not mean going to the gym, but I do mean being active. Go for a walk, go for a run or take twenty minutes every morning and exercise. Hold on; did you say you do not have twenty minutes a day? I am confident that you have even more than that. One way to find twenty minutes is to limit the time you spend online. This is just an idea.

If you want to find time, you will. Exercise, or some kind of activity, must become an integral part of your lifestyle.

DO NOT FEEL BAD THAT YOU HAVE MORE THAN OTHERS

When we have more than others, we sometimes feel bad. We feel as if we do not deserve it; we feel guilty. We feel as if we did not work hard enough for it. But the opposite is true. We deserve it!

We may have more than others because their time has not yet come. Maybe they have not done their part; maybe they have not worked hard enough. Whatever the reason, we should never feel guilty for what we have, assuming that we acquired it in an honest way and did not cheat or steal. Instead, we should be happy to be fortunate and use what we have to help others.

You probably know that nothing is for free. If there is no pain, there is no gain. So, if you have more than others, you must have done something to deserve it. Be proud of yourself, enjoy what you have and use some of your fortune to help others.

DREAM YOUR DREAM AND DREAM BIG

I want you to remember that nothing is impossible in this world. The sky is the limit. If you can dream it, you should always go after it.

The problem is that people stop dreaming when they reach a certain place in life; for example, getting to a certain age, starting a family or getting a job. This is so wrong. So many dreams remain unfulfilled if you stop. The dreams are there, but no one will claim them. And our life without dreams becomes a very dark place.

The more wishes and dreams you have, the more magnificent your life could become.

So, dream your dream and dream big!

SPEND TIME WITH YOURSELF ALONE

We always find enough time to spend with our family and friends, but we very often forget about ourselves. You need to start seeing yourself as you see others, set the same priorities and pay yourself the same attention. Your body, mind and soul will thank you.

Spending time with yourself alone is very important in today's hectic, fast-paced world. You need to spend alone time once in a while and do what only you like to do. You need to be "selfish" and make yourself a priority.

When I spend time with myself alone, I usually choose to be outside surrounded by nature. It allows me to absorb the energy from the trees, flowers and all of nature that surrounds me. The point here is to be alone and not be disturbed by anyone or anything.

Try it. You will quickly realize what you have been missing.

WE ALL ARE ONE

Black, white, brown, maybe green. Why does it even matter? We live in the twenty-first century, and it still seems to make a difference. Why? What is wrong with us?

We all are humans; we live on this planet together. We share this world. And we all make this world beautiful by being ourselves.

We need to respect each other and forget about our skin color, background or anything else that makes us seem different. We breathe the same air; in all of us, our blood is red in color. We are all brothers and sisters. We all are humans. We all are one.

NOT EVERYTHING THAT SPARKLES IS GOLD

This proverb is usually used in connection with material things. However, its essential meaning can be applied to just about anything: people, ideas, jobs, etc.

The point is that we can be easily tricked by something shiny - an exterior glitter or a first impression.

In order to learn about the true qualities of an object, for example, we need to get to know more about it. We should not judge it only by its exterior or our first impression. Would you be able to distinguish real gold from fake gold? Probably not, unless you tested it to see if it was genuine.

When you deal with someone or something for the first time, do not immediately assume that because the person or object looks shiny on the outside, you will find the same qualities on the inside. The fact that someone or something looks great at first does not guarantee that it will still look great once you learn more about it.

THE RICHER YOU ARE, THE NICER AND MORE HELPFUL YOU SHOULD BECOME

I believe that people continue to evolve and develop. I also believe that money can spoil your character, unless you appreciate, recognize and use its power the right way.

When someone does not have enough money, it does not make them less of a person than those who have more.

When you have more money than others, I again assume that you did not steal or cheat; you should, of course, enjoy it. Buy nice things, travel and have fun. Enjoy the fruits of your labor.

A part of your wealth - the amount of money is up to your discretion - should always be used to help others or to make others happy. Money should never spoil your character; it should improve it.

The more money you have, the nicer, wiser, more helpful and more sophisticated you should become.

MUSIC CAN HEAL

Music, especially classical music, can heal. The frequencies and vibrations enter your body and create inner harmony. The nicer the feelings that music evokes in you, the stronger the healing process can be.

Unfortunately, it goes the other way, too. The more violent and disturbing the music, the more it can cause you to feel ill.

The music played on TV or the radio is too aggressive today, and I honestly doubt it can have any healing properties. Everything you listen to affects your mind, soul and body.

In the past, cultures - such as Indian or African - would always give great importance to nice acoustic music because it had the power to heal, to relax and to uplift.

Always select music with a melody that pleases your ears. Close your eyes, sit back and listen. If the music gives you pleasure and brings tears of joy to your eyes, then most likely it will have the ability to heal you, as well.

NEVER CUT CORNERS OR GO FOR
THE EASY WAY

When we work on a project, we should always try to complete it to the best of our ability.

There will be times when a quick and convenient solution will suddenly appear and convince us that we can get by with less effort than we thought we needed. We might be tempted to omit a few steps and take a shortcut that will not be noticed by anyone. However, this route will not get us to the best outcome - the 100% outcome. You should know that if you cut corners, or go for the easy way out, this decision will one day catch up with you and you will have to deal with the same project or issue all over again, but it will be worse. It will most likely require more work than if you had put in all of the necessary effort the first time.

It is like baking a cake. You have all the ingredients, but in order to make it easier, you decide to skip one. Why not? No one can see; no one will ever know. So, you go for it. When you are done baking the cake, it looks great and you are sure it will be tasty. You take the first bite and quickly realize that the one ingredient you knowingly omitted is missing, making the cake tasteless.

This cake could one day be your job, your relationship or your education. If you do not do your very best at first, it will eventually come back to haunt you, costing you more time or more money later.

SUNRISE AND SUNSET: DISCOVER THEIR BEAUTY AND POWER

There is something magical about sunrise and sunset. Our predecessors knew it and found time to dedicate their full attention to those two special moments of the day.

Sunrise will give you energy for the day. Sunset will, on the other hand, calm you down so you can finish the day relaxed.

We do not always have the opportunity to watch sunrise or sunset, but when we do, we should always take advantage of it. Not only are these events beautiful sights, but they are also very powerful. Once you watch them, you will understand.

THE MORE LANGUAGES YOU KNOW, THE MORE HUMAN YOU ARE

Learning a new language makes your brain stronger. Even better are the opportunities your new language skills can provide.

I know four languages, some better than others. Whenever I have an opportunity to talk to someone in their native language, I do, assuming it is one the four I know. It creates a different momentum; it allows you to meet and get to know people in a different way. It opens doors to new friendships, experiences, opportunities and memories.

I know that some of you probably think that there is no need to learn a language, because today's technology allows us to translate one language into another effortlessly - you can do it on your smart phone. Believe me, it is a different experience when you actually speak the language. It is more fun.

Learning a new language is not easy, but when you do, you become a richer person. Plus, it has a very positive effect on your brain.

YOU CAN LEARN SOMETHING NEW FROM EVERY PERSON

Even though we might not like every person we meet, we can learn something new from everyone.

Every person knows something we do not for many reasons, including having a different background, age, culture or life experience.

I always try to listen to a person I meet very carefully. I observe the person and try to find out something interesting about them. I have never met anyone who hasn't taught me something new. Sometimes, I even learn something new about myself.

Start seeing other people as opportunities to learn new things. See them as walking fountains of wisdom, available for free. Try it; stay patient and open-minded. You will see that you can only benefit from it.

SOME THINGS JUST TAKE TIME AND PATIENCE

Throughout our lives, we will have many desires and goals, whether for an object or an accomplishment. Rest assured that most, if not all, desires will eventually be fulfilled. However, the timing may be different than you expect.

Most of our desires will not happen on our timeline. I have learned that certain things happen in our lives at the time they were meant to happen. It almost seems as if we must mature and grow up first in order to handle a desire becoming a reality.

Some of our desires will take more time, and some will magically occur when you least expect it. For all your desires, whether for a new car, a new house, a well-paid job or a spouse and children, there will be a right time. Believe me, all will be fulfilled at some point in your life.

Trust the timing of your life, and if something does not happen when you want, do not give up. It only means that the right time has not come yet.

EVERY DAY IS A GIFT

We all take our lives for granted. Most of the time, we don't think of life as anything special; we think we will live forever. Every day of our life is a gift, and it should be treated as one. We never know whether we will be given another day, so we should live each day as if it is our last.

Today's hectic lifestyle keeps our minds so preoccupied that each day seems only as long as a heartbeat. Very often, when people get older or approach the end of their lives, they say they would have slowed down so they could have enjoyed the beauty of every day.

Enjoy every sunrise and every sunset, listen to birds singing and look for ways to become a blessing in someone else's life.

Be grateful for your family and other people around you; be grateful for being healthy and lucky enough to wake up in the morning and have one more day in this beautiful world.

Never take even one day in your life for granted.

HUGGING TREES

I learned about hugging trees and the special power of trees from my mother.

Trees are so beautiful, so majestic, standing tall, always strong. They look like they are from another world.

Trees are full of energy; they have healing power. The best approach is to find a forest, walk through it, find a tree you like and hug it. Have only good intentions; trees have their own souls and can feel. Share your desires with them and let their energy enter your body.

I know it might sound funny when I tell you to go and hug some trees, but when you try it, you will understand what I mean.

Be open and nice to them. Hug them as if they were a part of your family (actually, they are). And do not forget to say thank you to them.

WALKING BAREFOOT

Like hugging trees, walking barefoot can at first sound silly. Please know that I am not suggesting walking barefoot to work or school, on the street or in a shopping center. I suggest, and strongly recommend, that you try walking barefoot, for a few minutes, in nature.

Find a beautiful meadow, take your shoes off and dive in. Start walking, close your eyes and feel the cool, soft grass under your feet. Then stop for a minute and imagine that you are becoming an undivided part of the nature surrounding you.

The best time to do this is in the summer, in the morning, while the morning dew is still on the grass. It is so refreshing and relaxing. Because there is nothing between your feet and the ground, you literally become one with the nature around you. It is very energizing, and again, it can heal your soul, mind and body.

THE ONLY DIET YOU NEED TO FOLLOW

First things first: nothing is for free. If there is no pain, there is no gain. There is no miracle pill or diet plan that can make you slim by itself. If there were, this chapter would be missing from this book.

People do not mind spending a fortune on all kinds of diets. Each one promises us the body of our dreams, and we fall for it. If you have tried one of those "miracle diets," you probably know by now that it really does not work.

I will tell you a well-known secret that everybody knows but many people ignore. If you follow this simple rule, your weight loss is guaranteed: Your daily calorie intake must always be less than your daily calorie expenditure. It's that easy. If you combine this eating plan with some kind of daily activity and drink plenty of pure water (two liters or more), which will help clean your body and get rid of fat faster, it is almost impossible not to lose weight.

Believe me, it is simple, it is free and it is suitable for almost everyone.

DO NOT LET YOUR SPIRIT GROW OLD

Getting older is a natural and unavoidable part of life. Everyone will eventually grow old. Our faces will wrinkle and our bodies will lose some of their muscle, but there is really no reason for our spirit to grow old.

I have seen men and women in their thirties who act as if they were in their sixties. I have seen men and women in their eighties who still enjoy life, are full of energy, have goals, dreams and bring joy to other people's lives. What is their secret?

The secret is that you should never allow your spirit to grow old. Being young does not mean only having a beautiful face and a strong body. Those are just exterior features. What matters is on the inside. We might not be in full control of our bodies when it comes to aging - at least not yet - but we are in full control of our spirit. So, keep your spirit young.

You are only as old as you feel on the inside. Believe me, your age is really just a number.

SLEEP AND THEN SLEEP SOME MORE

Sleep is very important at any age. Our minds and bodies need sleep to recover, to rest and to develop. It is a fact that people who get enough sleep are happier, healthier, more refreshed and are overall more successful.

We all live busy lives, always trying to find some extra time, but our sleep should be the last thing we sacrifice.

Sleep helps us stay focused and affects our mood. Everyone needs a different amount of sleep - some more, some less. We should, however, aim for six to eight hours of sleep each night. If you have the time, and feel like taking a nap during the day, do not feel bad; go for it!

EVERYTHING GOES BETTER WITH A SMILE

There must be something magical about a smile. Have you noticed that when you smile, everything becomes easier, people around you are nicer and you start feeling happier?

People around us are hungry to see a smile. A smile will open doors. A genuine smile will really work miracles. Try it and you will see.

A smile is contagious. When you smile at someone, that person will smile at you or someone else.

A genuine smile has the power to make people feel better, more cared for and more loved.

Still don't believe me? Well, how does it feel when someone greets you with a smile?

FIND TIME TO CELEBRATE AND HAVE FUN

Finding a reason to celebrate should never become difficult. If it does, and we start feeling like there is no reason to celebrate and have fun, we should seriously think about it and find out why.

The reason to celebrate does not always have to be a special occasion or a big event. We can celebrate anything we want. The more we celebrate and the more fun we have, the merrier our lives will be. People who have fun and are happy live longer and are generally more successful than others.

Be creative, and do not be limited only by holidays, birthdays or name days. Find a reason to celebrate everything you do, see or experience.

ABOUT THE AUTHOR

Dominik Prokop was born in 1979 in the magical city of Prague, former Czechoslovakia, where he spent most of his childhood before moving to the state of Maryland in the United States, where he still lives, works, writes and enjoys his family.

He is a successful entrepreneur, writer, humanist and international traveler. The wisdom contained in this book comes from learning about different cultures and meeting and listening to people all around the world, accepting them just the way they are.

He believes that each of us could contribute to creating a better world in which we all can live in peace and harmony.

NOTES

NOTES

CONTINUE YOUR QUEST FOR WISDOM AND HAPPINES

Join us again on a quest for wisdom and happiness!

Same as the first book in our 101 Life-Changing Principles trilogy, the Volume II. ...Now We Know, but We Want to Know More... & the Volume III. ...Tonight, Make the Stars Go Wild... of this book continue its legacy.

Legacy to inspire, motivate and provide an opportunity to create a better world. A world full of happiness, understanding and love.

Visit our website:
www.101publishingcompany.com

Like us on Facebook:
www.facebook.com/101publishingcompany

We would love to hear from you:
info@101publishingcompany.com

We misspelled *a word* on this page. We know where it is. Will *you* find it? We are not perfect...yet ☺

THE MUST-READ BOOK FOR PARENTS,
AND MOST IMPORTANTLY, FOR THEIR CHILDREN

101
LIFE-CHANGING PRINCIPLES
VOLUME III.

...TONIGHT, MAKE THE STARS GO WILD...

YOU WILL NEVER LEARN THIS AT SCHOOL!

DOMINIK PROKOP